Inspirational

Thoughts From

God

Bill Vandiver

Published by
Edge Productions
7028 Church Street E.
Brentwood, TN 37027
www.inspirationalthoughtsfromgod.com

a division of Fura Books

The Library of Congress Cataloging-in-Publication Data Applied For

William Vandiver—
Inspirational Thoughts from God

p.   cm
ISBN-13: 978-1-890224-15-8
1. Religion/Inspirational   2. Self-Help/Affirmations I. Title
2013

Printed in the United States of America

1 3 5 7 9 10 8 6 4 2

Book editing and design by
Lisa Wysocky, White Horse Enterprises, Inc.

For interviews or information regarding special discounts for
bulk purchases, please contact us at
bill@inspirationalthoughtsfromgod.com

Dedication:

To my dear friend Kathryn Kimble, who inspired me so much. I know you are giving all the ladies in Heaven make-overs! I miss you daily!

Acknowledgements

I wrote this book after enduring one of the most trying times of my life. During this time I had many conversations with God, and He instructed me to write down His inspirational thoughts. I didn't realize in the beginning exactly what I was writing down, I just did as I was told to do. I continued to write until one day He told me that "this book" was done. He has since reminded me daily to "finish the book," and now I have. All of the inspirational thoughts in this book are from God.

Huge thanks must go to my mother, Ann Vandiver; my sister, Beth Hollis; my brother, Dwight Vandiver; my best friend, Randall Odom; my Philly BFF Tiffany Lahn; and a person who has encouraged me tremendously, Charles Scarbro. I also owe so much of who I am to my dearly departed father, David Vandiver. Not a day goes by that I don't think of him, or something he said!

I want to acknowledge my holstic doctor of twelve years Dr. Larry Rawdon and his wife, Rita. His compassion, caring and knowledge of what God wants for the human body never ceases to amaze me. I want to thank my surgeon, Dr. Kyle Mannion; my oncologist, Dr. Jill Gilbert; my radiation oncologist, Dr. Anthony Cmelak; my medical doctors, Dr. Depender Bal and Dr. Reisman; Michael Skinner, DDS and Richard Sullivan, DDS for their amazing dental skills; Jenny Gibbs, my dental hygienist of over fifteen years; my acupuncturist, Dr. Chongbin; Dr. Andre Lagrange, my neurologist and epilepsy specialist; Dr. Olalekan O. Oluwole, who discovered amazing things about my blood; my personal trainer (who encouraged me to get up and get going on the worst of days) Josh Williams; and my massage therapist, Enoc, who made the worst days seem better!

I was so fortunate to be able to put together a group of medical and health professionals who were willing to communicate with each other and work toward my best interest. You are all amazing human beings and I'm so thankful God put each of you in my life! Also, a big shout out to all the amazing nurses and staff at Vanderbilt Medical Center and all the staff at the Vanderbilt valet service for always having my car back to me ASAP! I also thank Cancer Treatment Centers of America for their advice.

Thanks also go to my dear friends Stacie Kinder, Rhonda Adkins, Jeanette Jolley, Connie Harrison, Rick Erwin, and Lolita Newland. A big special acknowledgment to Julia Nicholson: without her personal assistance I could not have accomplished many of the things that I did. She sat with me and listened the day I came home from the hospital and I remember feeling as if I was speaking with my own angel! Thanks to Joni Moore for her detail in spelling and proof reading; and to Jon and Wanda Nave, Irvin and Louise Rusk, and Richard and Cristine Millstein for sharing their natural God given talent with me so that my life and career would become what it is today! My talented staff at my salon, The Edge of Brentwood, support my efforts daily; as do all of my amazing clients (friends); my cousin Janice Pledge; and Dale Robble, pastor at Highland Park Church in Nashville. Tennessee. It is a daily reassurance to know that I can count on everyone's love, support, and enthusiasm. Thanks also to Lisa Wysocky for encouraging me to do this book and assisting with the finished project.

Most of all, I want to thank God for giving me the opportunity to write His thoughts. I hope I fulfill the remainder of my days on earth living up to His greatest expectations and doing the job He planned for me, long before I was even thought of!

I hope that at any time you will be able to open this book to any page and it will fulfill your need for inspiration. I find myself re-reading the thoughts often for continued encouragement and needed uplifting!

And lastly, this book is about God's messages. Proceeds from this book will be used to benefit Colby's Army, colbysarmy.org; the Middle Tennessee Epilepsy Foundation, epilsepytn.org; Safe Haven-Empowering Homeless Families, safehaven.org; Springboard Landings, springboardlandings.org; and other charitable organizations and purposeful causes. God told me this book was a platform for me, and a platform for what is to be seen, but I know He has a plan!

Please visit inspirationalthoughtsfromGod.com to read the entire story of how this book came to be!

Bill Vandiver
December 2013

The
answer to
ALL
problems
begins with
prayer!

Very
dramatic
people can
bring lots of
drama to
your
life!

It's
not what is in
your house or
what it looks
like, its ONLY
about the love
that resides in it!

Always

seek the best that

life has to offer,

but be prepared

for valleys and

peaks. Those

valleys make the

view from the

peaks AMAZING!

Remove
the words "entitled"
and "deserve" from
your vocabulary.

Everything in life is a
gift, not an
entitlement or
reward.

THERE
SHOULD BE
TREMENDOUS
MORE PLEASURE
IN GIVING THAN
GETTING.

IF THERE IS NOT, REEVALUATE
WHAT YOU SEE
IN THE
MIRROR.

Always
seek to like what
you see in the
mirror.

Try to look
everyday!

**If
something brings
you happiness that
doesn't cause you
harm or sin, do not
put more credit into
what others think,
but more into what
you know!**

When
GOD created you in
his vision he didn't
compare you to
others in the making.
He has sole purpose
for you!

Ask

GOD

everyDAy

tO help

shOw yOu

his purpOse

FOR YOU

anD hOw tO

best serve

Him!

Accomplishments
in life that make YOU proud are
not always what GOD had in
store for you, but those
accomplishments may help you
realize that later in life!

Start
and end
everyday
with a
prayer!

*Is
there a correct
way to pray?*

*Yes, from your
heart!*

You
may not enjoy
every person
that you
encounter, but
try to find a bit
of love for
them in your
heart.

Until

you take the time to

get to really know

someone there is no

way to really know

what is going on in

their life, so don't be

too quick to decide

someone's place in

your life until you

know their story.

Try
to do all things out of
love!

Life is
meant to
be lived,
and lived
is what you
define it
to be!

**There's
one "thing" that
no "amount of
money" in the
world will allow
you to
purchase . . . time!**

"Make
GOD
a part of your
life
EVERYDAY in
SOMEWAY!"

Live
EVERYDAY in the
moment, and reduce the
amount of time you
spend living in the
future!

It
must be done, but
don't forget to enjoy
the time you are living
in right now!

THE FASTEST ROAD TO FAILURE IS TO STRIVE FOR PERFECTION.

*Always
strive to do
your best, not
to be the best*

The
"best" is
nothing
more than a
matter of
opinion!

Always
giving more than
expected and
always being okay
with receiving less
than anticipated will
always allow you to
remain humble!

The

word "humble" is a

wonderful adjective

when people talk

about you, and a

wonderful noun if it

honestly describes

you.

I'm

writing this book,

I hope it will help me

to continue to become the

person that I know GOD

made me to be.

My failures arrive every minute, my blessings arrive every second!

I

don't ever expect

to get this thing

called life right,

but I would be

disappointed

with myself if I

quit trying!

Good

and bad flow

through the same

atmosphere,

which is why we

must constantly

ask for GOD'S

strength.

The

higher you connect with

GOD, the farther it

seems you fall when

you sin. Thank you

God for catching me each

time I fall.

I
lived fifty-one years
before I found out that
I should ask GOD what
he wanted me to do
that was pleasing to
him.

Daily, "He" now gives
me that direction and
all along I thought "I"
was so amazing!

Live
everyday
within your
means and
live everyday
to fulfill your
dreams!

Your dreams are GOD inspired thoughts!

Are

frustrating

situations that

occur in your

life the result

of your poor

decisions?

Without

ever having bad

things occur in your

life you would never

truly appreciate how

wonderful life is.

Let people help make your life better with their strengths!

Things
don't always go
as planned, but
things always
go as they
should!

If
you find the Bible
difficult to
comprehend, then
find a version that
suits your way
of learning!

**Pray
to God, have
faith in GOD,
and then put
into action
what he instills
in you to do!**

Pray
about all
decisions that
you
make!

We
all say phrases
such as
"everything
happens for a
reason" but yet we
still use words like
"coincidence" and
"accident."

DON'T
EVER ALLOW
YOURSELF TO FEEL
ASHAMED,
EMBARRASSED, OR
INTIMIDATED BY
GOD.

HE
WOULD NOT WANT
YOU TO DO THAT.

You
needn't wait
until you are in a
bad position or
need something
to reach out to
GOD.

He is there
all the time.

If
you believe
that you reap
what you sow,
then always
try to sow
great grass!

Make

the foundation

of your life

based on

qualities, not

quantities.

Delivering your
BEST
is a
Choice!

Excellence
is a state of
mind that you
should always
expect of
yourself.

If
you allow
GOD
to become your one true
love, and connect with
GOD,
then you are at a place
where you can be
forgiven of sin because
being a sinner is
inevitable.

I'm

certain that God is

not sharing anything

with me that He is

not willing to share

with everyone. I am honored

that He asks me to

write it down.

Sometimes
people who really love
you will tell you things
that you need to hear but
do not want to hear.

Always
try to step back to
evaluate what they say!

How
do you view
issues: as a
problem or a
challenge?

**Everything
from the
moment you
open your eyes
to the moment
you go to sleep
is a blessing!**

Our

bodies can survive on

very little. It's society

and socialization that

makes us think we

need more than we

do!

There will never be more than

24 hours in a day,

7 days in a week,

365 days in a year.

Don't spend your time wishing you
had more time. Spend your time being
thankful for the time you have!

Because

you want to

better your

life doesn't

mean you

think you are

better than

others!

Don't try to spend your life being the best, just try to spend your life doing your best!

Knowing

the difference

between your

"wants"

and your

"needs"

could be the secret

for you to have more

time to spend with

GOD!

Try
not to wake up
every day and
think about what
you want.

Try
to wake up and
think about what
you can do!

If

you live your life

with GOD, death is

nothing more than

an extended

vacation until you

see your friends

and family again.

You
know how to
call GOD—
his number is
P-R-A-Y!

**Take
time for
GOD
everyday.**

A
purposeful
life is a life
with
direction!

The
same minute that you
experience when you
are twelve is the same
sixty seconds that you
experience at fifty.

The
reason that it seems so
much faster is due to
clutter and stress!

Make
time every
day to speak
to
GOD,
but take more
time every
day to LISTEN
to GOD!

YOUR

personal well being starts

with you and ends with you.

YOU

must decide that GOD has

made you the most important

person in your life.

YOU

Putting yourself first allows

you to take care of others!

Don't
ride other's trains,
Be
the
train!

You
can be a leader
while being a
follower.
Supporting the
leader with 100
percent of all you
have is being a
leader while also
being a follower.

**GOD
does not fear
Satan.**

**If
you put your faith
and trust in GOD
you should not
fear Satan either.**

Before
you ask
Others,
ask GOD
FIRST!

Love
and respect
of others are
two of the
greatest gifts
in the world.

Start
every day off
with a plan, and
do not allow
distractions to
interrupt it.

Greed,
not money,
can be the
source of
many
problems.

Can
someone ever make
enough money?

Define
"enough" and there
lies the answer to
this question!

Each

person's definition of

success is different, so

don't judge others

because of their

ideas!

**Everything
started
from
an
idea!**

There is "art" to every simple little thing in life!

There

is no shame in

being successful, as

long as you

obtained it without

stepping on anyone

or anything to

acquire it!

Just

be happy.

You would

be surprised

how easy it is

:)

If

you allow everything to

be in GOD's hands and

out of your control, you

will find that your

personal list of

disappointments will be

very small!

Stop

trying to do

GOD's work!

GOD
has an
incredible
sense of
humor; don't
be so serious!

GOD
LOVES
CHILDLIKE
BEHAVIOR
IN RESPONSIBLE
LIKE ADULTS!

NEVER
FORGET HOW TO
PLAY, LAUGH
AND HAVE FUN.

IT
DOESN'T COST
ANYTHING TO DO
THAT!

Create
a list of your wants.

Now
make a list of your needs.

Look
at the difference to see
how much LESS stressful
it is to live in your needs
and not in your wants!

There

is nothing wrong

with wanting

things, as long as

getting them

doesn't require

additional stress to

you or someone

you know.

*Stop
trying to
be perfect. You
are driving
everyone around
you crazy!*

LIVING
A LIE IS LIKE A ROTTEN
EGG IN THE CARTON,
EVENTUALLY IT WILL
COME OUT AND
EVERYONE WILL
SMELL IT!

Life

will never stop changing so

embrace it and see what is

around the next bend. You

might find that it is

amazing!

It's
your life and your
choice to either try to
do it yourself, or turn
it over to the one who
created you and allow
Him to help you make
the best of it.

Know who you are and be okay with that.

Is
what you are about
to do or say going to
harm someone in
some way.

If
so it could
potentially harm
you!

Simple doesn't mean boring. It means uncomplicated!

If

you truly believe

GOD is the creator

of everything good

and bad, then don't

allow yourself to be

the judge of good

and bad.

Acceptance
can be like a
horse pill, hard to
swallow but it
can be lifesaving.

If
a person
of a color or lifestyle
that is not to your
liking was the only
person available to
save your life, would
you ask them to do it?
Or would you die
hating them for being
how they were born?

Have
you ever
seen a child
about to do something
wrong? They usually look
left and right to see if
anyone is looking. Funny
how such a young, small
brain knows the difference
between right and wrong.

The
difference between right
and wrong is not between
the pages of a book, but
between your ears and
somewhere in your chest.

(Your heart, silly.)

Don't
tell someone
you will say a
prayer for them
and then don't,
or that you have
said a prayer for
them and you
haven't!

It's

more

important to

believe you are

somebody than to

ACT like you are

somebody!

A thought or an idea is a message from GOD!

No
matter how
large or small
any task seems,
getting it done is
an
accomplishment!

You
do not have to attend
church to have a
relationship with GOD.

A
church is a place to have
a relationship with other
people who may or may
not have a relationship
with GOD!

Don't
feel bad about
yourself if you don't
attend church.

Feel
great about yourself if
you have faith in
GOD!

Positive
energy
is
contagious.

Negative
energy
is
destructive.

Every
thought has
consequences
and everything
occurs through
the power of
GOD!

Criticism
is

GOD's

way to
direct you
one way or the
other!

Make every second count, or account for something!

Sometimes doing nothing is doing something!

When
choosing to do
nothing, allow that to
be your time to talk
with God.

That
then becomes the
most important thing
you did!

Multi-tasking

is great, but remember

to focus on ONE thing at a

time!

Search
until you find something
positive about all bad—

It's
there and you may have to
get really creative to find
it—

maybe
even imagine it, but find
it!

Who
am I to write this
book?

I
am a believer of
GOD, a sinner, and
he asked me to do
it!

That's
who I am to write
this book!

**Keep
reading until you find
at least**

1 thing

you need in this book!

**Maybe
that is what God
wanted you to read
and me to write!**

To
get inspired,
it helps to put yourself
in an inspirational
environment and
surround yourself with
inspirational people!

Webster's

dictionary defines

love as:

an intense feeling

of deep affection

**Loving
someone doesn't mean
believing everything
they believe in.**

**It
means being there if
and when they need
you!**

If
you feel the
need to control,
then get over
it! That job was
taken years ago
and GOD has no
plans to retire!

If
your life is off track,
whose fault is it?

Were
there not choices
placed in front of you?

Don't
blame God for your lack
of judgement.

ALL
CHOICES can be
revised by GOD
through PRAYER!

Why
does the word
GOD cause
some people to
flinch or
become
uncomfortable?

WRITE
YOUR
OWN
BOOK.

EVERYONE
HAS
A
STORY!

EVERYONE'S
LIFE IS A GREAT
STORY.

HOW
MANY PAGES WILL
YOUR LIFE'S STORY
CONTAIN?

Fill in the blanks:

A negative person / environment makes me feel_____.

A positive person / environment makes me feel_____.

After I commit a sin I feel

_____.

After I ask for forgiveness from God I feel_____.

Don't
try to justify
everything. It is not
always for you to
understand.

Keep
a note taking method at
hand at all times.

You
never know when GOD will
send you an inspiration that
you need to jot down!

**Are
you trying to get GOD
on your schedule, or do
you allow yourself time
to get on GOD's
schedule?**

Good – God = 0

(Borrowed from a church lawn sign,

but I love it and had to use it!)

Never

stop being

a kid at heart no

matter how old

you get,

just grow

up!

GOD
will come into
everyone's life.

He
will work through you
if you allow him to.

GIVE

YOUR LIFE TO

GOD,

JUST AS

JESUS

GAVE HIS LIFE FOR

YOU!

Don't be afraid or ashamed to be a child of GOD!

**Stay
alert, you
never want to
miss what you
were meant
to see or
hear !**

THE
THREE BEST
SOURCES TO FIND
GOD:
THE BIBLE,
YOUR HEART,
AND PRAYER!

Have
a plan for every day.
Plan time with God, to
exercise, to be with family,
to maybe do nothing.

Sometimes
doing nothing is doing
exactly what you need.

There
are 168 hours
in a week. **If you sleep
a minimum of 56
hours, exercise a
minimum of 7 hours
and work a minimum
of 40 hours that leaves
you 168 hours to be
with GOD!**

Isn't
a challenge
nothing more
than a request
from GOD that
puts you out of
your box?

Don't
compare what
GOD is asking
you to do to what
he is asking others
to do.

When
you see your
reflection in the
mirror, do you see:

A)Your physical appearance,

B)What others see in you,

C)The respect,or lack of, that
you are giving to the Body
that GOD gave to you!

or

D) All of the above

Your
heart and soul can
be seen by others,
felt by you, and
directed by GOD

We
are all a result of
OUR choices.
Sometimes
the answer to our
choices is no to all or
yes to all, or yes to
some and no to some.

There
is no shame
in the word
NO!

No

is a word

that can be used in

a positive way!

**Saying
NO
is not always a bad
thing.
:)**

Always
know that GOD has
an arm in your
arm, a hand in
your hand, and a
shoulder to lean
on. He is always
there.
See it?
He is love.

**Don't
allow other people
and/or situations
get in the way or
change your
feeling about YOUR
relationship with
GOD.**

Not

all

choices

are

easy!

Bad
choices can
seem more
lucrative and
glamorous than
good ones!

Every
person has a
purpose in life.

That
purpose can
change and is
between them
and GOD.

Your

partner or

soulmate should

be someone who

provides you joy

and happiness in

your darkest time

of need.

Try
Always to
make sure your
glass has more
being put into it
than mouths
drinking from it!

GOD
will
lead
you
to

inspiration!

satan

provides you

with negative

choices, and

GOD provides

you with

choices.

What
is the source of your
choices, and who
benefits once you
make it?

Weigh
that thought before
you make a decision.

Have
you ever
considered the
pain GOD
must have felt
because he
wanted to
save your
soul?

**Take
ten seconds to
pray about every
choice you make.**

**Ask
God to bless your
food to your body.**

**Make
both a habit!**

**Live
each day
fearlessly.
GOD is with you!**

Love is Visual

Love is Visual

Love is Visual

Love is Visual

Love is Visual

Love is Visual

Love is Visual

Love is Visual

As far as the eye can see!

ONE
YEAR AGO I
COULD BARELY
PUT A JIG SAW
PUZZLE
TOGETHER, AND
NOW BY A
MIRACLE OF GOD
I HAVE WRITTEN
THIS BOOK!

To
see love
you need
to BE love.

If
you think that your talks
with GOD are in your head
know this:

All
things come from GOD,
even your thoughts.
So now,
reconsider that thought!

**Finding
5 in your everyday
life on a scale of 0 - 10
may be easy, but
maintaining 5 in your
every day life on a
scale of 0 - 10 is
difficult and a
challenge!**

God
is
Good
ALL
the
Time!

Rest

is purposeful,

and how much

you need is

between you

and GOD.

If

putting

yourself in bad

places can produce

bad results, it stands

to reason that putting

yourself in GOD's presence

could produce Godly

results!

If
you have the ability to think
yourself sick doesn't it
stand to reason that you
can think yourself well?
Try it.

The
power of positive thinking
is absolutely amazing.

Daily,
I have to remind
myself to not sweat
the small stuff, it just
eats up positive
energy that others
or I might need to
help fix something
really important!

Being
who you are, what you
are, and where you are
is irrelevant.

Who
you help, how you
helped, and where you
are going will
determine your
accomplishments in
life.

We
can become in life
whatever we desire. It
just depends on how
strong your desire is
to fulfill your will.

The
quality of life that
the people around
you experience
could be a result of
something you did.

Respect

Love

Peace

Happiness

Acceptance

Love thy neighbor!

**Love
starts from
within, and many
people lack so
much in loving
themselves that
they have little
love to give.**

It
starts with
each of us doing
our best for each
person we
encounter
each
day.

Do
not allow the
very small percent of
bad things or
people get the
larger percent
of your spirit and
love!

SMALL
MINDS NEED A
SMALL SPACE,
BUT BIG MINDS
NEED CONTINUAL
ROOM TO GROW!

**If
living life one way
produces certain
results doesn't it
make sense that
making an about
face will produce
the opposite
result!**

**Every
corner you turn leads you
to another choice.**

**If
you have made an
incorrect choice, just
turn around and head in
the opposite direction.**

Life
is the biggest
gift in the
world, so
unwrap it
slowly!

We
all breathe and
bleed. Does that
make us all equal?

Yes,
but does it mean
we all have to be
the same?

No!

We
all come into this
earth with obstacles
and challenges that we
must over come.

Each
of us has our own
obstacles and many are
not visible.

Don't
compare your challenges
with others. You might
be surprised how lovely
you have it!

Knowing

your

weakness

is

your

greatest

strength!

An
ego must take
energy from
others to grow.

A
positive attitude
must be given
to others to
flourish!

An
attitude is when
you know you
are good.

An
ego is when you
think you are
good.

When
you put something "out
there" you can look like a
braggart, a liar, or a
visionary. It's all in the
presentation and the
follow through.

I
find putting it out there
challenges me to make it
happen, because I want to
be true to my word.

When
you have
the least to
give is the time
to give your most!

Life

is all about quality,

not quantity.

Inspiration comes from everywhere, but you must have your eyes open to see it.

"It" and "they"
are two of the most
powerful words because
it and they mean so
many different things to
so many different
people!

For a person who is ninty years old means there have been 32,850 "day" pieces of the puzzle of life.

We all know that one piece of a puzzle doesn't create a picture and that it is vital to complete the entire project.

In essence, that person's one piece represents 1/90th of his or her yearly life, or a small scene within the puzzle of life.

But it is going to take all 32,850 pieces to create the entire puzzle of life that in turn creates a beautiful picture that could never have been foreseen by only looking at the one piece.

Take every day as it comes because only GOD knows the final picture before it is put together.

Just
as life has evolved, so has
GOD.

GOD
is the source of all things so
don't think of GOD as an old
man.

God
<u>is the forever, the past, the</u>
<u>present, and the future.</u>

Staying

focused on

something

constructive can be

more difficult than

staying focused on

something of no

meaning or

purpose.

GOD

blessed you with a
brain. Don't
insult him by not
using it.

God
is in your heart
and at times Satan
wants to use your
brain.

Always
trust your
heart; it's God
talking to you!

Cream will always rise to the top.
Oil will always separate from water.
Heat will always rise to the ceiling.

These are the laws of nature.

We are all aware that you can't change or
disobey them, so why do we continually
try to change or disobey the laws of
nature with respect to life.

Right is right, wrong is wrong!

**The
only time
it's too late to
change is one
split second after
you die!**

Why
put off being your best,
giving your best and
enjoying all the wonderful
things of life?

There
are so many
chapters of life.
What chapter
will your life
write next?

Stop
blaming.

Get a mirror and start

changing

to what you want to see looking
back at you!

If
GOD puts a
moment in front
of you to do
something great,
take it!

If
you have to lie to
convince yourself
that you should do
something, then you
either shouldn't do it
or you should work
on your self
confidence.

**If
you can
"arrive" once
you can arrive
time and time
again!**

Everyone
has their "moment",
some at nine, some at
ninty-nine and some
in between. Maybe
some more than once!

Don't
stop untill you
experience the
moment(s) GOD has
planned!

ANYTIME

YOU

LEARN

YOU

GROW!

If
you don't think you
have a purpose,
keep searching and
it will one day
appear—maybe
without you even
seeing it coming!

**Today's
purpose
in life will be
tomorrow's story
to tell others that
might inspire them
during their time
of need!**

Go
through
challenges in life
and come out on
the other side then
say "problem, what
problem?"

Never
say never,
except to things
that are not
GOD blessed!

Some

people need to

experience GOD's

"should never do" list

so they can say **"been**

there done that" and

"don't want to do that

again!"

God
will talk with you,
but deaf ears can't
hear.

You
must open your
heart to hear!

Go
where life takes you,
someone there needs
YOU!

Just

simply

believe!

Keep
it
simple!

Bring
it
on!

Live life fully!

Create

Love

Cherish!

Open your mind!

Extend

your

heart!

Let

it

go!

Walk
with
GOD
daily!

I
am
a
blessing!

Pain

will

not

break

me!

Sometimes
the road to
somewhere
has to be
created!

Your
road
is
not
someone
else's!

Don't
be afraid to be out of
the box if you really
feel it's what you
are supposed to do!

Someone

always had to

be the first!

*Sometimes
the only way to know
the wrong way is to go
down that path.
Then, acknowledge,
turn around, and head
the right way!*

EVERY
PERSON AND
THEIR ACTIONS
ARE VITAL TO
THE DAY TO DAY
FLOW OF LIFE.

Take
life as seriously
as Jesus took
his. He had a
purpose and
stayed focused.

**Maybe
your purpose in
life was not meant
to be seen during
your lifetime.
Maybe it's on the
other side.**

Death
is inevitable.

Live
life each day full
strength, as if death
is right around the
corner 'cause it could
be.

Believe you can.

Believe you will.

Believe it is.

Believe it was.

You
know how you know
when someone is
listening? You can
sense it.

When
you pray, do you have
that same sense?

**What
is your definition of
important? I bet it
changes every time
something REALLY
important happens
to you.**

It's
okay to be
alone, you have
GOD to share
your energy
with.

Life
is not about what
you haven't done
or haven't seen.

It's
about what you
did, do, or caused.

Pain
can bring you closer to
GOD.

Is
that the reason for it?

Only
GOD knows.

Leave
the
judging
to
the
professional!

You

can't see electricity but

we believe in it and

can feel it.

Faith

is the same.

You

should believe in it

and feel it.

If
you will let GOD
do his job you
will find that
life is much
easier!

Stay
focused on
the things
that GOD has
inspired you
to do.

Sometimes we don't get what we think we should have.

God protects us from ourselves first!

Why
does something so
difficult as forgiving
someone come so hard?

Just
let it go and move on.

Don't
let other's wrongs against
you hold you back.

Are

you making a

passing grade in

the test of life?

All things that will
happen to you
today will
happen as a
result of your
blessings or
needs.

If
everyone was
a superstar,
who would
drive us to
the show?

If
you are a leader, be a
great leader.

If
you are a follower, be
a great follower.

Finding
your calling is GOD's
wish for you.

If

we were

all meant to be the

captain there would be

no sailors. But if there

were no sailors, there

would be no need for a

captain. Purpose is

everything!

Being
a great leader
means being able
to be a great
listener, a great
delegator, and a
great asker of
others!

Tackling
one task at
a time is like
eating one chip at
a time, eventually
you will complete
the entire bag!

Stay
purpose focused!

Purpose
focused produces
results!

Keeping
life simple is
a very
complicated
duty!

If
your space
doesn't stimulate
creativity and
purposeful
thinking, find a
creative and
purposeful
space!

Expect
the most from
yourself
so that you
can ask the
most from
others.

If
you are a
personality that
calls things as you
see them, remember
that not all things
are as they
appear!

A
big mistake
some make in life is
not taking chances
and opportunities
out of fear that they
might make a
mistake!

God
created me to
love, create,
motivate, and
help those
around me!

There

will be more

drama tomorrow

to replace what

you dealt with

today!

A

simple

life

is

a

life

with

direction!

Take

time for

everyday.

For us,
things don't
always go as we
planned but things
always go the way
GOD intended.

You
should never
"need" people in
your life, you
should only
"want" people in
your life!

A
star at the top of the tree
is beautiful to see but
hard to touch.

But,
a beautiful ornament
near the bottom of the
tree is both touchable
and beautiful!

Being
at the top is not always
being "ON" top!

**When
others place their
best interest in
front of you is
when you need to
know what is in
your best interest.**

We
are all created equal in
the eyes of GOD.

We
are all created from the
love of GOD.

Some
will experience more
opportunities, due to who
they are surrounded by,
but those opportunities do
not make them more
important in GOD's eyes!

If
you spend
your life
striving for
perfection you
will spend a
lot of your life
failing.

"God,
please keep me centered and focused."

"God,

please use me to do your work."

"God,

how can I impact someone's life in a positive way today?

"God,

thank you for today!"

"God,

I know at times
I think
questionable
thoughts about
you, please
forgive me and
strengthen my
faith."

"God,

please show me the way!"

"God,

I don't understand, Please help me."

"God,

thank you for
allowing my eyes
to open today!"

"God,

thank you for allowing me to be able to read and/or hear this message today."

All
GOD wants
from you today
is your best, not
to try to be the
best!

If you open
your heart to
GOD it will
become
capable of
love.

Faith
is doubting
something and
turning it over to
God, then not
doubting for a
split second that
it is in His hands!

Sometimes what appears to be bad things happening to good people is what God has in His plan.

The more time

you spend doing

all that life has

to offer, the

less time you

may have to

spend with God.

Balance!

Today
you awoke
because GOD has a
plan and a job
for YOU!

**Money
is not evil.**

**It's
what you choose to do
with it that can create
evil.**

Strange
isn't it, when something big,
really big and great happens to
us we exclaim "OMG" and
maybe "I can't believe this is
happening" with tears of joy.

When
something bad happens we
exclaim "OMG" and maybe "I
can't believe this is happening"
with tears of fear.

We
"thank him" and "scream out
to him" in our highest and
lowest moments of our lives

Please
don't see God
as an old idea, an old man,
a thing of the past. God is
fresh, he is now, he is
current, he is more in
touch with EVERYTHING
than any human being,
because He is the creator
of "the touch" and the
source of "everything."

Don't

allow your first

thoughts about something

bad happening to you to be

"Oh God, why me???!!!,"

Let it be "God, thank you

for being in my life and

working through me."

**It
takes getting
right with GOD
to get right
with life!**

The
ability to reach
around behind
yourself and touch
your butt is so that
you have the ability
to pick your butt up
when needed and
get it in gear!

Maybe
all the facts about
GOD are not published
but:
He is
He can
He will
and He does!

Don't
question little details, see
the big picture!

**Choose
to
radiate
positive
energy!**

The
deeper you dive into a pool,
the longer it takes to swim up
for air.

The
deeper you dive into sin and
trouble, the longer it takes to
get back up.

Just
as there is air at the top of the
pool, there is an amazing life
at the end of the road of sin.

Ever
notice you don't
get many things
unless you ask!

Today
God grant me peace
when I am trouble,
remove my pain when
I hurt, help me
trust you when I
doubt, and comfort
me when I cry.

POSITIVE
BEGINS WITH A "P"
FOR A REASON. IT IS
"POWERFUL!"

EVIL
BEGINS WITH AN "E"
FOR A REASON. IT IS
THE "END!"

Focusing on the positive will always drown out the evil!

Evil
gets
too
much
attention!

A
positive
mental attitude
is a healing
attitude!

The
three Ds:

Desire
Determination
Dedication

When
life gives you lots
of problems,
relish in them
because it means
you are alive.

IF
YOU ALLOW
YOURSELF TO BE PUT
IN A POSITION OF
STRESS YOU WILL
BECOME STRESSED!

God
has a plan for
all of us. Are
you allowing
him to do his
intentions?

Savor life.

Live life.

Cherish life!

Don't
let the bad
things that happen to you
daily get you down.
They are only bumps in the
road that will allow you to truly
appreciate where you are when
you are basking in all your
glory!

Every

road you travel

will have ups and

downs, twist and

turns, and bumps

and potholes. And

that is just the road.

Then there is life!

EVERY TIME YOU RELINQUISH YOUR BURDENS TO GOD THE WEIGHT IS TAKEN FROM YOUR BACK.

Don't
worry so much
about the
details, just have
faith in the
"ONE".

Would you prefer "cheese" with your "whine" or some champaign to toast your cheer!

Life
is about
disappointments
and glory.

Are
you gonna relish in
the happy moments,
or feast on the
disappointing ones?

GOD

can knock

and knock, but

if you don't let

him into your

house (heart)

then you are

missing the

greatest guest

ever!